"Performance management is about creating relationships and ensuring effective communication. It's about focusing on what organizations, managers, and employees need to succeed."

"Performance management is an investment up front so that you can just let your employees do their jobs."

_____

How to Manage Performance

24 Lessons for Improving Performance

ROBERT BACAL

MCGRAW-HILL

New York Chicago San Francisco Lisbon
London Madrid Mexico City Milan New Delhi
San Juan Seoul Singapore Sydney Toronto

The *McGraw-Hill* Companies

Copyright © 2004 by The McGraw-Hill Companies, Inc. Printed in the United States of America. Except as permitted under the United States Copyright Act of 1976, no part of this publication may be reproduced or distributed in any form or by any means, or stored in a data base or retrieval system, without the prior written permission of the publisher.

1 2 3 4 5 6 7 8 9 0 DOC/DOC 0 6 5 4 3

ISBN 0-07-143531-X

Printed and bound by R. R. Donnelley.

Developed and produced for McGraw-Hill by CWL Publishing Enterprises, Inc. Madison, Wisconsin, www.cwlpub.com.

McGraw-Hill books are available at special quantity discounts to use as premiums and sales promotions, or for use in corporate training programs. For more information, please write to the Director of Special Sales, Professional Publishing, McGraw-Hill, Two Penn Plaza, New York, NY 10121-2298. Or contact your local bookstore.

Contents

Managing performance   viii

Modernize your thinking   1

Identify the benefits   3

Manage performance   5

Work with employees   7

Plan precisely with clear goals   9

Align employee goals   11

Set performance incentives   13

Be approachable all year   15

Focus on communication   17

Make it face-to-face   19

Avoid rating perils   21

Don't rank employees   23

Prepare for the appraisal   25

Start reviews on the right foot   27

Identify causes   29

Recognize success   31

Use cooperative communication   33

Focus on behavior and results   35

Be specific about performance   37

Manage conflict with grace   39

Use progressive discipline   41

Document performance   43

Develop employees   45

Continuously improve your system   47

✓ Managing performance

Why should you care about managing the performance of your employees? Because communication between manager and employees is essential for increasing productivity, improving morale and motivation, and allowing coordination of each employee's work with the goals of the unit and the organization.

Many managers dislike performance management. They try to avoid it or they try to cut corners or they simply mess up. It's often because they don't understand performance management.

So, they're focusing on the wrong things. They focus on *appraisal* rather than *planning*. They focus on a *one-way flow of words* (manager to employee) rather than *dialogue*. They focus on *required forms* rather than *communication*. They focus on *blaming* rather than *solving problems*. They focus on the *past* rather than the *present* and the *future*.

So they waste time and effort and just don't get out of performance management the benefits that it can provide—if done properly. In fact, their time and efforts often only make the situation worse.

Performance management is an ongoing communication process, undertaken in partnership between an employee and his or her immediate supervisor, that involves establishing clear expectations and understanding about the following:

- the employee's essential job functions
- how the employee's job contributes to the goals of the organization
- what it means, in concrete terms, to do the job well

- how job performance will be measured
- what barriers hinder performance and how they can be minimized or eliminated
- how the employee and the supervisor will work together to improve the employee's performance

That's what these 24 lessons are all about.

Performance management is an investment up front so that you can just let your employees do their jobs. They'll know what they're expected to do, what decisions they can make on their own, how well they have to do their jobs, and when you need to be involved. Done properly, performance management can save you time and effort.

I can't give you recipes for success, because it's impossible to use a cookbook approach to managing performance. No one way will work for every manager with every employee in every situation.

I hope that you'll find in this little book principles and actions that will help you get more results from the time and effort you put into managing the performance of your employees. After going through these 24 lessons, you'll have a good grasp of performance management, so you can develop a way of doing it that helps you succeed at helping your employees succeed.

"Performance management is, in some ways, very simple and, in other ways, very complex. It consists of lots of parts and requires some skills. But if you approach it with the proper mindset, you can make it work—and pay great benefits."

☑ *Modernize your thinking*

*O*ne of the challenges of making performance management and appraisal work involves leaving behind older ideas of how work gets done, the roles of manager and employee, and the purposes associated with performance management. For example, managers who believe their role is to tell staff what to do rather than work with them to solve problems don't fare well with performance management. Managers who believe performance appraisal is the venue for bashing employees over the head don't do well. And managers who refuse to take on the role of helping everyone succeed quite simply don't get success.

There are two things to understand—what performance management should be and what performance management should not be. These aren't based on theories, but on observations of what works and doesn't work in real workplaces.

Performance management isn't a way to threaten, cajole, or intimidate employees into being more productive. It isn't a method to blame or find fault in employees. It's not for attacking the personality and attitudes of employees.

So, what is it? It's a broad set of tools used for the purpose of optimizing the success of each employee, each work unit, the manager, and the organization. If these goals are to be achieved, the manager must adopt a modern mindset.

Commit to the idea that your job is to build success in the present and future and not to manage by looking at the past (managing by looking in the rearview mirror). That means you must be looking forward.

Understand that the benefits you can achieve through performance management will come only when you complete all the steps, not just evaluating performance.

Accept the fact that, on your own, you can improve performance only a little bit. Employees, on their own, can improve performance only a little bit. However, when you and each employee realize you are on the same side and work together, then you can improve performance by huge amounts, not only for each employee, but also for your work unit.

Here are three other suggestions:

Invest: Performance management requires an investment on your part. Yes, that means you need to do the work. Most important, it means that if you invest the time and effort, you will save time, effort, and costs.

Share responsibility: The responsibility for productivity lies with you and the employee. For responsibility to be shared, there needs to be two-way communication between manager and employee. You need information to move things along. The employee needs information.

Seek out employee wisdom: Performance management is a good way to harness the knowledge, skills, and experience of employees. They do the work every day. They are closest to the action. Often they know better than you how to fix things.

"Employees need to play an active role in defining and redefining their jobs."

☑ *Identify the benefits*

*I*t's not surprising that managers tend to skip the performance management process. Most of us haven't had a chance to participate in performance management done properly. As a result, many don't understand the benefits for the employee, the manager, and the organization. Performance management can be valuable—provided you understand what it can do for you.

Performance management takes an upfront investment to achieve certain very practical aims. For example, performance management can be used to make sure each employee's work contributes to the work unit's goals. It can reduce the amount of "supervision" you need to provide by clarifying for employees what they need to do and why they need to do it. Performance management, properly done, allows you to identify problems when they occur so you can fix them early. The need to discipline is reduced as a result. The bottom line is that performance management can improve productivity—if you commit to the entire process. You'll recoup your investment.

Besides being the tool for improving productivity, performance management also protects you in situations where you fire an employee or have to make other difficult decisions about employees. Performance management involves documenting problems and communicating those problems to employees. If an employee files a complaint, your documentation will show that your decisions were based on performance issues and that the employee knew about those issues and had a chance to address them. Solid performance management documentation can even deter frivolous lawsuits and complaints.

Here are three ways to focus on the benefits you want:

Keep the goal in sight: Before any step into the performance management process, remind yourself that your goal is to improve performance and help everyone succeed. Focus on that and you will start seeing benefits quickly.

Be patient about results: You will see some benefits from the performance management process very quickly after starting. Performance planning, by itself, should help reduce wasted effort and the need to closely supervise your staff. The full benefits won't be obvious until you've been through the entire one-year cycle at least once or twice.

Do all the steps: Performance appraisals alone don't improve performance. When you do all the steps of performance management, that's when you get the payoff. Plan performance, communicate during the year, diagnose problems, and review performance.

"Since performance management helps employees understand what they should be doing and why, it gives them a degree of empowerment—the ability to make day-to-day decisions."

☐ **Appraise performance**

☑ *Manage performance*

*T*here's a major misconception about performance management. Many people confuse performance appraisal and performance management, believing they are one and the same. When employees and managers believe that performance management consists of one annual meeting where the manager evaluates performance for the purposes of punishing employees who don't make the grade, is it surprising that nobody looks forward to the process?

Performance evaluation is just a small part of performance management—and probably the least important part. To improve performance and create a more enjoyable workplace, you need to manage performance, not just evaluate it. If you just evaluate, chances are you'll end up with less productivity, not more.

So, do all the steps. Start out by planning performance. This critical step involves making sure both you and the employee understand what he or she must do in the next year to contribute to the overall goals of your work unit. Both of you should be clear about how the employee needs to do the job.

Make sure you communicate about performance all year round. That helps you identify and solve problems early before they result in significant costs.

Managing involves making the right decisions. What do you need to make those decisions? Data and information. Part of the overall performance management process involves observing and collecting data so you and the employee know how things are going.

Documenting is the process of recording significant discussions and events related to an employee's performance. Proper documentation (done during all stages of the process) makes performance discussions easier, since you and the employee don't have to rely solely on memory. Documentation may involve complex forms or it may be as simple as jotting down some notes.

Diagnosis and problem-solving refer to how you and the employee identify barriers to performance (past, present and future), so you can formulate plans to overcome those barriers.

Finally, there's the performance appraisal meeting, which yields a summary/review of the year. If you successfully complete all of the other steps, the review meeting is simply a fast formality, since everything would have been discussed during the year. That's why the actual performance appraisal meeting is the least important part of performance management.

Here are three important things to do:

Ensure that employees know the difference: Employees need to understand these steps. Explain the point of each part. Explain what will happen. Explain how the process will benefit them.

Make it two-way: Remember that performance management involves an exchange of information. You get and give information to the employee. The employee gets and gives information to you. That's how you improve performance.

Make it about you, too: Performance management isn't just about what the employee does. It's about identifying your role in improving performance. Talk about and decide how you can help, what you can do.

"If you believe that performance appraisal is performance management, it's just not going to work."

☐ **Tell employees**

☑ *Work with employees*

---

*Y*ou have a pretty good idea about what your employees are doing and need to be doing, right? Since that's the case, you could simply tell your employees what they need to do and then, at the end of the year, tell them how well they've done. A fair number of managers do just that. They feel they know best about the work that needs to be done.

But there's a problem: this approach doesn't work very well. Here's why.

Managers have one perspective about the work. Employees have another perspective. They complement each other and you need both. When you and your employees combine your knowledge, you improve performance.

Involve employees as equal contributors in the performance management process, particularly during performance planning, performance reviews, and problem solving. Not only will this make the best use of available information, but it will tell employees that you value their knowledge and insight. That's essential if employees are to become active and enthusiastic participants in performance management. Involvement also builds a sense of ownership and responsibility.

Treat employees, particularly experienced ones, as experts in their jobs until they demonstrate a lack of expertise. You do not have to agree with input from your employees and you're certainly not bound to act on it, but you should not dismiss it out of hand.

Guard against the tendency to rely on just your perspective, particularly when the goal is to identify why performance has been below expectations or how performance can be improved. Managers are often just too removed from the details of the job to have a good grasp of the source of work problems.

Here are three components to create a collaborative situation:

Give employees the information they need: Make sure employees have enough information about the goals and challenges your work unit faces. That helps them connect their own goals and work to those of the work unit. It allows them to be active, valuable, and informed partners in performance management.

Use more questions than statements: Encourage staff to share knowledge, information, and ideas by asking questions, rather than telling. Once their contributions are on the table, present yours. Questions about goals and objectives and questions that encourage self-evaluation are particularly valuable.

Listen, respond, and act: Don't ask for participation and then ignore what the employee says. Listen first—and then make sure the employee knows you're listening. Then respond with your own understanding and perspective. When necessary, commit to action to help improve performance—and then follow through on your commitment.

"If managers look at performance management as something they do to employees, confrontation is inevitable. If they view it as a partnership, they reduce confrontation."

☐ Don't bother with goals

☑ *Plan precisely with clear goals*

Do employees really know what they are supposed to accomplish? Do they know their goals? Yes and no. They probably know enough to do some of their job tasks well, but they probably don't know enough to become spectacular, self-directing, and self-monitoring.

Employees need to know what they're expected to do, the relative priorities of their various job responsibilities, how well they need to do their tasks, how their responsibilities link up with the work unit's goals, and—most important—how to tell if they're on track or not.

When employees have all this information, they can guide themselves and make day-to-day decisions without coming to you all the time. Since they know what success means and what might indicate problems, they can make corrections on their own or, at minimum, work with you to solve problems early. Clear goals also allow easier determination of whether or not the employee has hit the target at appraisal time.

During performance planning, work with the employee to set measurable goals/objectives and focus on employee behavior and/or the results the employee is to achieve. Use numbers and quantities when possible (e.g., less than three customer complaints a month, less than 1% defective parts). Goals can describe what you want (repeat customers) or what you don't want (customer complaints).

Goal setting is best done as a negotiated activity. If you've provided the employee with an understanding of his or her job, the employee can develop a preliminary set of goals. Don't tell. Start by asking what he or she thinks needs to be accomplished and how to measure accomplishments. Then negotiate if needed.

Here are three important tips for setting and using goals:

Change goals as needed: Things change fast. You may need to change goals as situations change. Don't feel locked into a set of goals you negotiated with an employee. If those goals no longer fit, revisit them and change them.

Focus on mutual understanding: You can focus too much on the details of the goals, trying to get them just right. What's more important is that you and the employee share the same understanding. Before you finish setting goals, have the employee restate the goals in his or her own words and compare them with your understanding.

Be practical: Setting clear measurable goals is good, but sometimes goals that are easy to measure are the least important. Be realistic and keep in mind that even the best goals aren't always perfectly measurable. Don't exclude important goals just because they're hard to measure.

"Manager and employee need to agree on what objectives are most important and which might be less so."

✓ *Align employee goals*

---

*T*he entire performance management process ends up as wasted effort if the employee's goals and job responsibilities are not directly linked to the goals and mission of the work unit, department, and organization. The reasoning is simple. Not only do employees have to do things well, but they also have to be doing the right things. It's your job to ensure that the employee's work contributes to the achievement of organizational goals.

How do you align employee goals with the goals of the organization? The main mechanism for doing this is the performance planning process. Here's how it should work.

Ideally your company should be doing some strategic and tactical planning so that the company has some clear targets. Those clear targets are distributed among the individual work units, so that each work unit ends up with a clear set of goals it must achieve. Those work-unit goals are used during the performance planning phase to determine the goals and objectives of each employee. It's best described as a cascading process.

The logic goes like this: if every employee achieves his or her goals, the work unit achieves the goals assigned to it, which in turn helps the organization hit overall targets.

Apart from optimizing overall performance, this process has another benefit. It helps employees put their jobs in an overall context. When they know how their jobs fit into the big picture, they're more likely to be more motivated and get more satisfaction out of doing their jobs. Understanding the work-unit goals also makes it easier for employees to make decisions that take into account those goals.

Here are three ways to align employee goals:

Begin with the big picture: Start the performance planning process by reviewing where the organization is going. Then review what the work-unit must achieve. Then discuss what the employee can do. Get significant employee input on how he or she can contribute.

Tweak the timing: Aligning goals this way means that organizational and work-unit planning need to happen before individual performance planning. Consider altering your performance management cycle so it aligns with the overall work-unit planning cycle. Don't be discouraged if the organization doesn't plan, since you can make best guesses.

Reinforce during reviews: At the end of the cycle (performance appraisal), don't forget to highlight individual accomplishments and how they've contributed to the larger goals. Reinforce the links. Employees who understand how they're contributing tend to feel more ownership and pride.

"Regardless of what the rest of the company does, many managers find it useful to set aside one day a year to meet with staff and identify what the unit needs to accomplish in the coming year."

☐ **Ignore motivation**

☑ *Set performance incentives*

*W*e know people work best when they a) have clear goals, b) believe they can achieve those goals, and c) know what they will receive when they achieve those goals. There are other factors involved in motivating employees, but these three simple aspects are very powerful.

Incentives are a bit different from rewards. An incentive is something that is specified in advance. A reward is received after the fact. For an incentive to motivate an employee, the employee must know about it in advance. The specification of incentives should be part of the performance planning process.

Don't make the mistake of assuming that incentives need to be of huge value. Yes, large financial bonuses can improve performance, but so can small bonuses or other kinds of benefits. Access to training, consideration for promotion, small pay raises, or even a nice dinner can serve as low-cost incentives. In fact, huge bonuses can have a negative effect if not implemented properly, since they can pit employee versus employee in the pursuit of significant financial gain. Huge bonuses are not as cost-effective as moderate ones.

There are two critical times with respect to incentives—setting up incentives and determining if the criteria have been met.

Setting up incentives is part of performance planning; determining whether goals have been achieved is part of performance appraisal. When planning incentives, negotiate with each employee. Whatever criteria you negotiate, make sure that the employee can reach them if he or she works hard and exceeds normal expectations about performance.

If you use criteria the employee cannot possibly reach, incentives are worthless. Salary pays for "normal performance." Incentives reward superior performance.

Here are some more tips:

Use group and individual criteria: If you can, link incentives to both individual success and work-unit or company success. The employee benefits from hitting his or her targets. The employee also benefits if the work unit or company hits its targets. Tying incentives to work-unit success can improve a sense that "we're in this together."

Individualize incentives: Incentives works only when the employee wants the benefit offered. Be prepared to negotiate incentives on an individual basis. If employees can choose their specific rewards, those choices are more powerful motivators.

Avoid vague criteria: Using vague criteria linked to incentives is a recipe for disaster. Specify clear goals that can be measured. Don't link incentives to vague ratings scales. Make sure you and the employee understand the criteria in the same way.

"Think of your job as helping each employee hit that target, make that extra money, or get that promotion."

☐ Stay aloof

☑ Be approachable all year

*O*ngoing communication throughout the year is the backbone of effective performance management. In fact, it's an essential part of good management, period. You need information all year long about what's going well, what's behind schedule, and potential or upcoming problems.

Ongoing communication happens in two ways. You initiate it—and that's something you must do—or the employee initiates it by coming to you when he or she needs help, when a problem occurs, or just to keep you informed. Your job is to create a climate so employees will come to you with the information you need to help them and so you know what's going on.

You must create a climate that supports and encourages employees to communicate with you. How do you do that?

First, employees will come to you when they believe that you'll respond to news (both good and bad) in helpful and supportive ways. If employees believe that whoever comes to you with a problem will be blamed or harangued, they'll simply stop talking to you.

Second, employees will come to you when they know there's value in doing so. When you prove to employees that you will act to clear away barriers—and not just talk about it, deal with problems constructively, and make their lives easier—they will talk to you.

Third, how you behave when an employee approaches you is going to determine whether he or she comes back. If you send non-verbal signals that you are bothered by their "intrusion," employees will realize that no matter what you say about having an "open door policy," it's all phony. When approached, be attentive or, if the timing isn't great, set a time when you can have the discussion—and commit to it.

Here's more on staying approachable:

Explain what you need: Employees can't know what information you need or when you might feel they're bothering you with issues they could handle themselves. Explain the kinds of information you need and when it's a good idea for them to come to you with problems. Explain how you can help them with problems.

Listen: When approached, focus your attention on what the employee is saying. Don't do other things during the discussion. Use active listening, rephrasing and feeding back what the employee said. Prove you believe the employee's message is important—as it is to him or her.

Act: Listening isn't enough to ensure employees will come to you. Words are important but so is action. Employees will come to you if you are of some use, because you're prepared to act to solve problems if necessary. So, listen, respond, and then act. If you help, they'll share information with you.

"Aim all communication at identifying and solving problems, not blaming."

☐ Focus on the forms

☑ *Focus on communication*

*F*orms don't improve performance. People working together improve performance.

That's a point that's often lost in the minds of both managers and human resource staff who supply evaluation forms for use by managers. The truth is that most appraisal forms are so bad they make employees resentful and are far too general to achieve the goals and generate the benefits of performance management.

During appraisals, filling out the form is the least important part of the process. What is important is that you and the employee have a meaningful dialogue about past performance and what can be done to improve performance in the future (regardless of current levels).

What do you do if you are forced to use a form that is too general and vague and doesn't require recording information needed to improve performance? Complete the form if you are required to do so—but augment it in two ways.

First, don't limit your discussion to the form and its items. In fact, don't even bring out the form until the end of the meeting. Talk about the job, past performance, barriers to performance, and ways to overcome those barriers. Ask how you can help improve performance.

Second, you can document (write down) the important aspects of that discussion and append them to the form. Record any strategies or plans to improve. Include what you can do to help. You want to succeed in improving performance in spite of being forced to use a horrible tool.

Keep the following in mind:

Use forms to summarize, not tyrannize: When given a form, people tend to fill it out and provide only what it asks for. As a result, the form controls the review process, when you and the employee should be guiding the process. Use the form to summarize discussions and add notes to the form as necessary.

Lobby for better tools: Some appraisal forms are so bad that completing them will inevitably end up insulting employees. This happens if the forms ask for evaluations about attitudes and personality, rather than behaviors and results, or force you to rate a certain percentage of staff as below average. See if you can convince decision-makers to allow you to use a more flexible approach.

Focus on communication: Performance management is about communication. Even if you have to use poor forms, you can overcome the negative effects by being open and honest and working with employees to improve performance. Dialogue is the key.

"When you focus on performance management as a way of communicating and building relationships, the actual format of the reporting system becomes less important."

✓ *Make it face-to-face*

*F*or years, managers focusing too much on the forms have destroyed performance management. Now we have a new wrinkle—the use of technology for performance management. Various computer-based systems have been developed to make the process faster. One system literally allows you to "phone in" your employee ratings using a touchtone phone!

Here's the problem. Computers are great for recording large amounts of information and automating certain kinds of repetitive tasks. They do not, however, make the users of the technology wiser or smarter or improve their judgment and thinking abilities. They also do not improve communication abilities. And we know that these things are the essentials that make performance management work.

As with forms, people tend to do only what computer programs ask of them. Use a performance management computer program and people will do only what it requires. And that's not enough to improve performance.

Use the technology, but keep in mind the payoff comes from good face-to-face communication. Never allow any computer program to result in less interaction between you and your employees. Use technology for storing relevant information and data and for summarizing discussions you have directly with employees.

Keep in mind that technology allows us to do things faster. That's not always a good thing. If we do the wrong things, but do them faster, we get to the wrong place more quickly. When systems are automated, the resulting automating system will be only as good as the thinking that went into creating it.

Here are a few tips for harnessing technology:

Avoid technology tyranny: Don't restrict yourself to filling in online forms or doing only what's asked. Does it make sense to be told what to do by a machine? No.

Watch for poor setup: Performance management software usually needs to be customized to be useful. That customization is often done by information technology or human resource departments. Their needs are different from yours. The software can be tweaked, so provide feedback to improve it.

Fight the novelty: Don't be seduced by the novelty of these systems. It may be "cool" to sit by yourself and do performance appraisals on a computer. That doesn't mean it's going to get you where you want to go.

"Any method can have undesirable side effects, particularly if it's used without proper thought and care. Be alert to potential problems with your appraisal system."

Rate and run

✓ Avoid rating perils

*I*f you're using a rating form in your performance appraisals, it's best to be aware of their limitations and do your best to reduce their negative aspects.

Typically, a rating system has some sort of verbal descriptor (e.g., "completes tasks on time," "exhibits leadership ability"). For each descriptor, the rater is asked to assign a number (usually one to five) that best describes the employee's performance on that item. Variations include replacing numbers with evaluative phrases (e.g., "poor," "excellent") or combining the two. Often the exact same form is used to evaluate employees across a wide range of jobs. The items tend to be quite general.

That's the first problem. Because the items are so general, a rating doesn't give the employee enough specific information to improve. How does it help an employee to know that he or she is a "two"? It doesn't. In fact, it's likely to insult the employee, since nobody believes he or she is a two on a five-point scale.

Ratings are not usually tied to specific behaviors, so the ratings are exceedingly subjective. The numbers may make things seem objective (we're suckers for numbers), but they aren't. When these numbers/ratings are used to make personnel decisions, the subjectivity involved creates a huge conflict point.

Can you minimize these and other problems associated with ratings? Yes.

In a performance appraisal, never begin discussing a topic with the rating. Discuss the performance first. Once that's done, then negotiate a rating. For example, for "being on time," discuss instances where the employee has been on time or not, using any data you have. Identify the causes of any late arrivals. Only once you and the employee have done that should you choose a rating.

Here are three ways to minimize rating problems:

Be open about limitations: Employees understand the limitations of rating. They still need to hear that you understand the limitations. Explain that you realize ratings are a very vague way of evaluating. Treat them as fallible—and let the employee know that's your stance.

Negotiate ratings: Since ratings have very little objective meaning, negotiate the final rating for each item; don't just tell your rating. Don't get picky. Whether an employee gets a "three" or a "four" is not very important. Arguing over small differences creates bad feelings that affect future performance.

Don't sum ratings: Adding up the ratings to obtain a total overall rating of performance is meaningless. Don't do it. It's like adding up the numbers on football jerseys to determine which team is better. For a number of reasons—some simple, some statistical—adding up the items is unfair and inaccurate.

"Always clarify the meaning of each rating item before doing the rating. Discuss your idea of its meaning and ask the employee about how he or she understands it."

☑ *Don't rank employees*

Ranking employees as a measure of their productivity is not common. Where ranking is used, it's almost always misused and it should be eliminated.

That's a bit counterintuitive. You'd think it would be possible to look at 10 employees doing the same job and determine which is the best, then next best, and so on, all the way down to the worst. But you can't do this meaningfully and you can't eliminate ranking perils.

Is ranking ever appropriate? Yes. Where employees are expected to create one or two very specific results and they can be measured accurately, ratings can be used. A real estate agent could be evaluated in terms of a very few criteria—number of sales, dollar value, number of new clients secured. If that's all you care about, ranking can work. But what about the agent who interferes with other agents through cutthroat practices? Maybe you expect the agent to do more than sell, to contribute in other ways to the success of the company. Ranking then becomes a problem.

Ranking creates a win-lose situation among employees. There can be only one "best performer," only one "second best," and one "worst performer." So, for an employee to be the best, he or she can either become more productive ... or work to bring down the performance of everyone else. You do not want to create that kind of unpleasant competition, unless there is simply no need for employees to work together.

Finally, using ranking to make decisions about which employees keep their jobs is bad business. If you hire the right people, everyone should be performing well ... even the worst in your rankings. If you were to replace the bottom 20% each year, the chances are the people you hired to replace them would be worse.

There's no way to eliminate the problems with ranking systems, but here are three things to keep in mind:

Understand the faults: Ranking shows only relative contributions, at best. Rankings do not tell you the actual value of an employee. A low rank, when a person is performing well, may lower future performance.

Lobby for change: If you're required to use ranking, consider trying to get the requirement changed. Ranking ties your hands and your ability to make managerial decisions. It rarely succeeds. Companies that appear to succeed using employee ranking are succeeding for reasons completely unrelated to rankings.

Augment: If you must use rankings, augment them with elements that make performance management work. Plan performance and set clear objectives. Communicate all year long and problem-solve. Help everyone succeed.

"In the short run, ranking systems can encourage some people to work harder .... But they can also encourage people to passively or actively interfere with the work of others."

☑ *Prepare for the appraisal*

*T*here are few things worse than being involved in a performance review meeting when one or both parties don't know why they are there, don't understand the point, and haven't done any thinking or background work. Your goal is to limit the length of the actual appraisal meeting to about an hour, tops. If you go longer than that, fatigue sets in. Along with fatigue comes aggravation. So, you need to lay the groundwork beforehand.

There are two aspects to appraisal preparation. You prepare to play a lead role during the meeting in a way that encourages the employee to participate actively. The employee prepares so he or she can participate actively.

Preparation begins at the time you schedule the review meeting. Explain the purpose of the appraisal discussion and what to expect and outline any decisions that need to be made by the end of the meeting. You can discuss specific steps to help the employee prepare. You might ask him or her to review relevant documents—job descriptions, performance planning documents, and strategic planning and relevant documentation created throughout the year. Ask the employee to go through his or her objectives and make notes about whether he or she has achieved them or not.

It's good to provide some reassurance at this time. "I promise there won't be any surprises during the meeting" is a good phrase. What's important is that the employee begin to think about the things the two of you are going to discuss. Make sure you ask if the employee has any questions about the meeting.

Your preparation depends on a number of factors, including the forms you have to complete, your style, and the particular details of your performance management system. Review the employee's job description, job responsibilities, performance plans, and relevant documentation. Be sure to review the form you're expected to use. Make sure you understand it and think about how you'll use it to stimulate discussion. It's also a good idea to write a quick informal agenda outlining the critical steps you want to complete. You can share this with the employee at the start of the review.

Here are three simple activities that can help:

Get the participatory mindset: A few minutes before the meeting, remind yourself that you're there to create a dialogue. Commit to asking questions. Plan to foster self-evaluation. Promise yourself not to get into the blame game.

Touch base: A day or so before the meeting, confirm the appointment with the employee. Answer any questions. Verify that both you and the employee will be ready.

Prepare in person: Reduce anxiety about the performance review by preparing face to face. Don't do it by memo. That's far too impersonal and very intimidating for the employee. Schedule and explain in person.

"Arrange not to be interrupted. Have your phone calls held. This is the employee's time. Make it quality time."

✔ *Start reviews on the right foot*

*I*t's review time. The employee walks in. You both sit down. Then what?

Do you simply jump right in with "So, how do you think you did last year?" No, that's not how you start.

Understand that most employees are going to feel nervous about appraisal meetings, even if they have no negative experiences with you personally. That's because employees have had bad experiences in the past, perhaps years ago. Your first task is to create a climate in which the employee feels comfortable and understands you aren't there to beat him or her over the head with every little thing that's gone wrong. Here's how.

Welcome the employee as you would any guest in your office. The first few minutes can be social—small talk, if you like. Consider it a quick warm-up.

Then, to make the transition from social talk to talk about performance, here's a great beginning: "So, Mary, how are you feeling about this meeting?" Encourage the employee to communicate any anxiety so you can reassure him or her.

From that starting point, discuss or review and confirm the purpose of the meeting, how it will be conducted and the importance of doing this together. Be sure to focus on how the performance management and appraisal process can help the employee achieve his or her job goals.

Reiterate that there will be no surprises for the employee. If you have a brief agenda, you can share it. Once you've done that, end this portion with a question like "Does that make sense?" or "Do you have any suggestions to make this more useful to you?"

Here are three other tips for setting a positive climate.

Follow through during the meeting: Make sure you don't lose the positive momentum you create at the start of the meeting. Continue inviting the person to talk. Make sure you don't become overbearing or start lecturing. Focus on dialogue.

Share your feelings: In any situation, you can put a person at ease by sharing your own nervousness or anxiety.

Don't wait until it's too late: Create a positive relationship throughout the year, not just at the beginning of the performance review. If you treat the employee badly during the year, it'll be too late to change things for the meeting. Pay attention to your own behavior all year.

"Keep in mind that most employees have had unpleasant experiences with performance appraisals ... and will tend to see appraisals as a 'me vs. you' situation. Keep sending the message about what the meeting is for."

☐ Ignore the whys

☑ *Identify causes*

When you take your car to a mechanic because it's not working properly, what happens? Once the symptoms have been identified (e.g., squeaks, won't start), the next step is to discover why it squeaks or why it won't start. Without knowing the cause(s) of the problem, the mechanic must rely on trial-and-error. Swap one part and then see if it solves the problem. That gets mighty expensive and trial-and-error comes with no guarantee that the cause(s) of the problem will be identified so it can be fixed.

It's no different with human performance. Whether you must fix a performance problem or optimize a performance that's already good, identify what factors limit performance.

First, describe the problem as accurately as possible. When does less than desirable performance occur? Under what circumstances? For example, performance may be fine when the employee has a light workload, but errors may increase rapidly as the workload increases. Knowing that will help you find the root cause. Use questions and your own observations and available data to nail down the specifics. Don't forget that the employee is the closest to the action.

Second, ask the essential question—"Why?" If we call the performance problem "X," ask, "Why is X happening?" If you think, "A is the cause of X," then ask, "What causes A?" Track backward until you can't continue.

Here are three tips for identifying causes:

Look at multiple causes: Many things don't have a single cause, but a number of causes that feed into each other. Don't stop looking just because you think you've found a cause. Look for other contributing factors. The more causes you can identify and rectify, the more likely performance will jump.

Search everywhere: Managers tend to look for causes within the employee. Performance problems can lead directly back to the employee, but often performance is limited by things beyond the employee's control. Poor tools, poor planning, and inadequate resources are just a few things that can contribute to making performance less than optimal. Look far and wide for causes.

Use hypotheses: Treat your conclusions as hypotheses, not etched in stone. The proof that you have the right cause lies in addressing the cause. Then observe the impact on employee behavior and results. If improvement doesn't happen, repeat the cycle.

"The real payoff comes from identifying why performance succeeds when it succeeds and why performance fails when it fails, and then figuring out how to do more of the right stuff and less of the wrong stuff."

☐ **Praise grudgingly**

☑ *Recognize success*

Some managers who consider themselves "hardnosed" believe it's not necessary to praise employees and acknowledge their successes. They believe that salary is enough and "coddling" employees is unnecessary. They are dead wrong.

All of us need to know that our work and our successes are noticed, recognized, and appreciated. Salaries don't convey that sense to employees. If your employees feel you do not recognize their contributions, they won't go to the wall for you.

Recognizing success can take many forms—perks, awards, and bonuses are examples. The most practical forms of praise don't have to cost a cent, though. Look for instances where an employee is doing a good job. Then, when you find them, tell him or her.

Don't limit recognition to any time, place, or situation. You can recognize contributions over coffee, in team meetings, and in one-to-one-meetings. You can show your appreciation during all the phases of performance management: during performance planning, any time during the year, and, of course, during the performance review meetings.

There's no limit on praise, but be sincere and specific and accurate when you recognize performance. Sincerity is critical, since research suggests that when an employee believes you're rewarding or recognizing to manipulate him or her into higher performance, performance tends to drop, not rise.

Congratulate employees on special accomplishments, dealing with tough situations, and even regular run-of-the-mill success. But keep in mind that if you praise everything, employees will devalue your praise. Make sure you demonstrate an accurate understanding about the particular accomplishment. For example, if you congratulate an employee on always getting to work on time, but the employee has actually been late five times during the past month, you look like a fool who doesn't know what's going on.

Here are three pillars of employee recognition:

Explain the good: Acknowledging success in a general way is a good thing. It's even better if you explain exactly what the employee did well and why it was valuable. That accomplishes two things. It tells the employee what to continue to do and it provides a little motivational lift.

Catch employees doing good: Get out of your office to see what's going on and talk to staff. Look actively for successes rather than for problems. When you find an employee doing something good, comment and recognize that accomplishment on the spot.

Recognize with small rewards: When acknowledging accomplishments with some sort of tangible reward, use rewards of token value. Small rewards (e.g., certificate, plaque, small gift certificate, congratulatory coffee mug) don't result in bad feelings or destructive competition for rewards. Recognition rewards are best served in a context of fun and goodwill.

"Celebrate successes as they occur."

☑ *Use cooperative communication*

Some managers believe that the best way to "motivate" employees is to get in their faces or "read the riot act." That's not true. Fear is not a good motivator. The harder you lean, the more likely the employee will resent you and resist you. Aggressive talk breeds aggression.

By using cooperative language, you'll reduce conflict and send the message that you and the employee are "on the same side."

Avoid comments and criticism that can be construed as personal attacks. For example, "You aren't listening" and "You don't know what you are talking about" are personal attacks. Replace these kinds of statements with more cooperative language. For example, "Let's slow down a bit so we make sure we understand what each of us is saying" or "I'm not understanding your thinking here. Could you explain a bit more?"

Eliminate focusing on the past and using past-centered comments. For example, "For years, you've been late in getting your work done" is a past-centered comment that's likely to create an argument. Why? Because it's in the past and can't be changed. It's OK to refer to past events in passing, but not to focus on the past. For example, "I can recall a few instances where projects have been delayed. Let's talk about how we can prevent that in the future" is much more constructive and less likely to start fights.

Eliminate guilt-inducing phrases, comments that are meant to make an employee feel guilty, such as "If you really cared about this team, you would work harder" or "I guess you don't care much about this project." If you use these kinds of phrases, employees will fight you tooth and nail because they are inferences on your part and far too vague.

Here are three more tips on improving your communication:

Reduce unsolicited advice: There are times to offer advice and times not to. You have a right to make suggestions, but it's best to ask first. For example, "I have some suggestions about [topic]. Can we talk about them?"

Reduce commands: You also have a right to order or command that an employee do what you want. However, overuse tends to foster resistance and rebellion. Usually you can send the same message without being overbearing. "Get this on my desk today" is a command, while "I need this today; does that work for you?" is not.

Don't overstate: If you use words like "always," "never," "every time," and "all the time," you're overstating your point. People tend to fight overstatements. Overstatements are almost always inaccurate and intended to "win."

"Ask your staff, 'Are there things that I do or say that make you feel uncomfortable talking to me?'"

☑ *Focus on behavior and results*

Most people believe an employee's attitude and personality influence success at work. Every day we see people with different attitudes, some good and some bad. It seems that people with good attitudes are better workers. So, doesn't it make sense to appraise people's attitudes?

The answer is mostly no. Here's why. Attitude cannot be observed directly. You can't point to an attitude and say, "There it is … a bad attitude." You can't hear it, touch it, smell it, or see it. You can only infer it. And that inference, that conclusion about attitude, says as much about the observer as it does about the person under observation. You can't prove a person has a good or bad attitude, except to point to specific examples of behavior that you're taking as evidence of an attitude. Likewise, an employee cannot prove he or she has a good attitude.

The bottom line is that conclusions about a person's attitudes or personality are very subjective—and people are very easily offended when their attitudes or personalities are attacked. Focusing on them almost never results in improved performance. It's just a great way to create bad feelings.

Your primary concern should be to improve productivity and performance. Performance and productivity occur as a result of employees' behavior. Skip the attitudes. Skip the amateur psychology. Focus on behavior and results, preferably those that can be seen, heard, counted, and documented.

Here are a few important points about attitude:

Translate "attitude" into behavioral observations: You think, "John's attitude is affecting his work." Translate this into behavior by asking, "What behaviors suggest to me that John has an attitude problem?" (e.g., lateness, arguing). Then, when talking to John, talk about the lateness or the arguing (behaviors) and don't even mention attitude.

Translate personality attacks: When you tell someone he or she is "too aggressive" or "too passive" or make similar comments about personality, anger and resistance result. Translate those general comments into concrete examples. For instance, "Last week I noticed you seemed hesitant to ask Fred some tough questions. Did you feel uncomfortable?"

Think, "Will it help?" Remember: you want to improve performance, not start a huge war by insulting someone. Determine whether what you want to say will help or not by asking yourself, "Will my comments be specific enough and non-threatening enough to help the employee improve?" If the answer is no, find a better way to approach the issue.

"Distinguish between what you observe and what you infer. This distinction is very important."

☑ *Be specific about performance*

*W*e know beyond a shadow of a doubt that people need specific information about their job performance to improve. When that information is missing, performance tends to drop over time, even for better performers.

What kind of information do employees need?

- Specific information about what they are doing well and should continue doing
- Specific information about what they should not do
- Specific information about what they should do—instead of what they should not do

How specific does the information need to be? Here are examples of comments too vague to help an employee learn and improve: "You aren't selling enough," "You're too argumentative during team meetings," and "You need to work harder."

Here are examples of comments that are specific: "You might be able to improve your sales if you qualify your customers by ...," "I think you seem argumentative in team meetings because you tend to interrupt others," and "I've noticed that you get into work late about once a week and that prevents customers from contacting you in the morning."

The vague comments may in fact be true, but by themselves they are simply too inaccurate to improve performance, while the more specific ones are clear about what's needed—try this qualifying technique, stop interrupting, and arrive on time.

Here are three techniques to help you keep appraisal discussions concrete and specific:

Rely on specific examples: Use specific examples of behavior when talking about performance. For example, "In June I received three calls from customers unable to get in touch with you because you hadn't arrived by 9 o'clock" or "In the last team meeting, you interrupted Jane three times."

Stick to observations and facts, not inferences: Observations are things you see. Facts are about things you know, based on data (e.g., sale figures, customer comments). Inferences are conclusions, usually about an employee's attitude or personality. Avoid inferences and statements like "You're lazy," "You need to work harder," and "You're not a team player."

Make and use informal notes: You can't always talk about a performance issue immediately. When you do see things about an employee's performance that you want to mention later, make some short notes so you can be specific during the discussion. Use them to jog your memory.

"Employees need regular, specific feedback on their job performances. They need to know where they are excelling and where they could improve. If they don't know ..., how can they get better?"

☑ *Manage conflict with grace*

Disagreement and conflict are normal in any relationship where both parties care about the issues. In fact, you should worry if there's never conflict or disagreement. An absence of conflict can mean that the employee may not be committed enough to his or her job to stand up for the things he or she believes in.

Managers tend to fear conflict during the performance management process. If you prepare appropriately and handle performance management properly, you can significantly reduce the frequency and seriousness of disagreement.

You can't eliminate conflict, though. That's OK, because conflict can be a starting point for finding solutions that neither you nor the employee could create without the stimulation of disagreement. Whether disagreement results in constructive solutions or causes damage depends on how the disagreement is handled.

When disagreements occur, repress the urge to use your power as a manager to make a unilateral decision too quickly. Explore the employee's position. Truly try to understand the employee's point of view before you respond—and certainly before you make any kind of unilateral decision.

Here's a critical aspect of harnessing the power of disagreement. Make sure you don't do or say anything that will escalate the disagreement unnecessarily. Anything you say that is perceived as a personal attack or as an attempt to disparage the employee will escalate the conflict. That doesn't mean you can't make comments about performance problems, but you must stick to facts and observations, not inferences about character, intelligence, diligence, and other personal traits. Use concrete examples.

When managing conflict, here are some tips:

Use power as a last resort: Recognize that you have less power than you think. Overuse it and employees may rebel. You can always make a unilateral decision if it turns out that dialogue and negotiation do not succeed.

Consider timing: When emotions run high, that's the time to consider taking a break from the discussion—10 minutes, an hour or two, or even a day or two. Upset people do not problem-solve well. Anger creates anger, so be prepared to break the emotional cycle.

Show that you're open-minded: Employees react more favorably when they feel you're willing to listen and see their points of view. Recognize that each of you has a right to an opinion and should be heard. Showing open-mindedness contributes to the perception that you are also fair. Fairness breeds loyalty, not aggression.

"When confrontation occurs or becomes ugly, it's often because managers have avoided dealing with a problem until it's severe. Early identification of problems helps in the resolution process."

☑ *Use progressive discipline*

*A*lthough it's not among the main reasons for managing performance, performance management is an important tool for disciplining an employee. Discipline is not quite the same as punishment. Punishment has an "I will hurt you" quality, while discipline is the process of holding an employee accountable for his or her actions by specifying consequences that will be applied under some very specific circumstances. And, of course, discipline is applying those consequences when needed.

There are times when employee actions are so extreme or unacceptable that they require immediate action (e.g., assault, theft, gross safety violations). However, most disciplinary action related to performance does not require that immediacy. Enter progressive discipline.

There are several components to progressive discipline. First, you identify aspects of performance that must change. Second, you determine what will happen if that change does not happen by a specific time—the consequences (e.g., probation, demotion, suspension). Third, you communicate (and document) the information to the employee. Fourth, you reevaluate at the identified time. Fifth, you apply the consequence.

Usually the consequences themselves are progressive: you start with the most gentle consequences and then, if those are not sufficient to help solve the problem, you escalate. You may go through the cycle several times, depending on the value of the employee, the severity of the problem, and other factors that fit the situation.

Here are three suggestions to help you make progressive discipline work:

Problem-solve first: Discipline of any sort should be considered a last resort. You have an investment in each employee, an investment that you do not want to lose. Before you move to discipline, work with the employee to identify why the problem is occurring and try to help him or her overcome it. If that fails, discipline may be appropriate.

Weigh the consequences: Disciplining an employee means crossing a bridge that you may never be able to uncross. Disciplinary action can destroy any chance of a positive relationship between you and the employee. Also, before you decide to proceed, consider the costs of disciplinary action—the cost of replacement and the effect on other staff.

Identify, communicate, provide opportunity, and help: Give employees reasonable time to improve, except in very severe situations. Be clear about what they need to change and take an active role in helping them improve. First, be a "teacher/helper." Then, if helping doesn't work, be a boss.

"Any disciplinary action must be documented completely, in detail—the actual performance gap, how it was identified, how it was communicated to the employee, and steps taken to resolve the problem."

☑ *Document performance*

*P*erformance appraisal forms should not become the focus of performance appraisals. But that doesn't mean you shouldn't record important information about performance and document the essentials of any performance-related discussions you have with any employee. Documentation can be formal (records that are kept as a permanent or semi-permanent part of the employee's file) or informal (notes about performance used as memory joggers and usually not kept).

Document to provide an ongoing, fact-based record of both positives and negatives of employee performance so you can use that information in making decisions and avoid relying on memory. Documentation is also used to improve communication between you and each employee and to summarize any important discussions you have about performance. Writing things down helps both parties determine if they understand the discussions in the same way. You should use notes (informal documentation) to capture specific aspects of performance that occur during the year. Use those notes during the appraisal meeting.

Strong documentation offers some protection for you in situations where an employee feels you discriminated against him or her illegally. When you have a factual record of performance issues, you can defend job-related decisions that an employee might contest. You receive additional protection if you can prove that you gave the employee ample notice to improve prior to taking disciplinary action.

At the minimum, you need a record of goals and objectives set during performance planning, significant conversations about performance that occur during the year, and a summary of performance review meetings. Record commitments that you and/or the employee make, agreements that you reach, and anything else that either of you deems as necessary to improve performance.

Here are three important hints for documenting properly:

Sign off: Any formal documentation should be signed by both employee and manager. The employee's signature does not indicate he or she concurs with the content of the document. It merely acknowledges that he or she has seen the document. Make sure you explain this to the employee.

Document essentials: Write down what's important, but don't go crazy. Documentation should summarize. The exception to this is if you are proceeding with disciplinary action. In this case, your documentation should be more extensive.

Let employees comment: In the interest of fairness, allow employees to add comments to any formal document. If they disagree with the content, they deserve the right to have their disagreement recorded. Allow employees some time to draft their comments before the document is finalized.

"Documentation ensures that important information doesn't get lost. It's also important for legal reasons. Disciplinary action without proper documentation can be very costly."

☐ **Ignore skill development**

☑ *Develop employees*

---

*C*onsider that you already have a significant investment in your employees. It took time and money to hire them and get them up to speed. It makes sense to invest further by helping them develop and to improve their skills and, therefore, their ability to contribute over the long term.

Skill development is appropriate when you believe performance can be improved if the employee acquires or refreshes job-related skills. Skill development can also be used in cases where an employee might be suitable for increased responsibility or a promotion. Some managers use development opportunities, such as going to conferences and seminars as rewards for good performance.

How does this fit with performance management? Performance management provides you with the tools for determining whether employee development is indicated and what kind of development best fits the situation.

For example, use performance planning to identify possible barriers to goal achievement and identify what an employee needs to learn to achieve the goals. Performance appraisals can highlight gaps between where an employee is and where he or she needs to go.

Employee development need not be costly. You can use seminars and training workshops, but there are other alternatives. For example, you can pair up a less skilled employee with a willing, more skilled employee. You can coach the employee yourself if you have the required knowledge and skills. You can arrange for job rotations so the employee learns new skills and becomes a more adaptable part of your organization. Don't restrict yourself to just the more formal learning opportunities, such as training seminars. Informal ways of learning are often more effective and less costly.

Below are three suggestions to help you optimize staff development:

Follow up: Learning happens best when there is follow-up. If an employee goes to training, suggest reporting to other staff members what he or she has learned or meeting with you. Talking about learning reinforces the learning.

Link learning to goals: People learn best when they understand the purpose. Regardless of the learning methods, make sure employees understand how they'll use what they've learned. Tie development to specific goals or career enhancement.

Incorporate a development plan: The best times to plan for skill development occur during performance planning and performance appraisal. During both phases, discuss skill development goals and how to reach them. Document any agreements and commitments for the employee and yourself.

"In a constantly changing workplace, the skills needed for employee success change over time."

☑ *Continuously improve your system*

One of the mysteries of the world is why some decision-makers are completely oblivious to the total failure of their performance management systems, while all the others—managers and employees— understand the system is valueless. When decision-makers finally decide to improve the system, the new way ends up working like the old way, except with cosmetic changes. Who pays? Everyone.

Even though you may not be able to improve the overall corporate system, you do control the elements that determine whether performance management fails or succeeds. How you augment the corporate system, how you communicate with employees, and your overall management philosophy are just a few of the factors you can control. But you need to consciously evaluate your performance management system, so you can diagnose it and come up with ways to make it better.

Where to start? First, identify what you want the system to do. What are its primary goals? Next, find out whether those goals are being achieved. If the performance management system is functioning "below capacity," determine why. Then problem-solve to identify ways to tweak the way you do things. In other words, apply the exact same process to evaluate and improve the system as you use to evaluate and improve individual performance.

You won't be able to answer these questions by yourself. Your perceptions are important, but it's absolutely necessary to involve your employees in the evaluation and improvement process. Ask them.

You may also want to talk to your boss and to the human resource staff to find out how they feel about the success of the process and how it could be improved.

If possible, collect before-and-after data to assess how any changes you make are working. For example, if you modify how often you communicate with your employees, you might want to monitor whether some particular target function improves (e.g., lower error rates, less sick days).

Here are three pointers to apply to continuous improvement:

Evaluate the system every year: As part of your performance management process, make sure you ask employees to evaluate the process. Is it working for them? Is it helping them do a better job? What changes could make it better?

Understand perspectives: Employees, managers, senior executives, and human resource staff have different perspectives on whether the system is working. Often they are in disagreement. Recognize that the performance management system may seem to work from where you sit, but may seem like a disaster from where the employee sits.

Aim for small improvements: Improve your system continuously and incrementally, particularly if you cannot control the overall system. Small improvements build momentum. They quickly add up to better results.

"A poor performance management system undermines the credibility of management."

"Performance management is an ongoing process throughout the year. It's not just about performance appraisal. In fact, performance appraisal is only a small part of it. Performance management is about preventing and solving problems."

"Performance management is about people, communication, dialogue, and working together, not about forms or forcing employees to produce."

Other Titles in the McGraw-Hill Professional Education Series

The Welch Way: 24 Lessons from the World's Greatest CEO
by Jeffrey A. Krames (0-07-138750-1)
Quickly learn some of Jack Welch's winning management practices in 24 basic lessons. A great way to introduce yourself and your employees to the principles that made Jack Welch one of the most successful CEOs ever.

The Lombardi Rules: 26 Lessons from Vince Lombardi—the World's Greatest Coach
by Vince Lombardi, Jr. (0-07-141108-9)
A quick course on the rules of leadership behind Coach Vince Lombardi and how anyone can use them to achieve extraordinary results.

How to Motivate Every Employee: 24 Proven Tactics to Spark Productivity in the Workplace
by Anne Bruce (0-07-141333-2)
By a master motivator and speaker, quickly reviews practical ways you can turn on employees and enhance their performance and your own.

The New Manager's Handbook: 24 Lessons for Mastering Your New Role
by Morey Stettner (0-07-141334-0)
By the author of the best-selling title on the same subject from the Briefcase Books series, here are 24 quick, sensible, and easy-to-implement practices to help new managers succeed from day one.

The Powell Principles: 24 Lessons from Colin Powell, a Legendary Leader
by Oren Harari (0-07-141109-7)
Colin Powell's success as a leader is universally acknowledged. Quickly learn his approach to leadership and the methods he uses to move people and achieve goals.

Dealing with Difficult People: 24 Lessons for Bringing Out the Best in Everyone
by Rick Brinkman and Rick Kirschner (0-07-141641-2)
Learn the 10 types of problem people and how to effectively respond to them to improve communication and collaboration.

Leadership When the Heat's On: 24 Lessons in High Performance Management
by Danny Cox with John Hoover (0-07-141406-1)
From an F-16 pilot and nationally-known speaker, learn 24 lessons for effectively leading a diverse group of employees in a wide variety of situations.

Why Customers Don't Do What You Want Them to Do: 24 Solutions for Overcoming Common Selling Problems
by Ferdinand Fournies (0-07-141750-8)
Learn how to deal with sales problems from a best-selling author and master sales trainer.

How to Manage Performance
Order Form

1–99 copies	_____	copies @ $7.95 per book
100–499 copies	_____	copies @ $7.75 per book
500–999 copies	_____	copies @ $7.50 per book
1,000–2,499 copies	_____	copies @ $7.25 per book
2,500–4,999 copies	_____	copies @ $7.00 per book
5,000–9,999 copies	_____	copies @ $6.50 per book
10,000 or more copies	_____	copies @ $6.00 per book

Name _____

Title _____

Organization _____

Phone (_____)_____

Street address _____

City/State (Country) _____ Zip _____

Fax (_____)_____

Purchase order number (if applicable) _____

Applicable sales tax, shipping and handling will be added.

☐ VISA   ☐ MasterCard   ☐ American Express

Account number _____ Exp. date _____

Signature _____

Or call 1-800-842-3075
Corporate, Industry, & Government Sales

The McGraw-Hill Companies, Inc.
2 Penn Plaza
New York, NY 10121-2298